Natural Quarry

A JOURNEY ACROSS THE U.S.

David Boag

AGGREGATE
INDUSTRIES

Designed and published by Group Corporate Communications, Aggregate Industries plc

Printed and bound by Butler and Tanner Ltd, Frome

Foreword

In 1999 we commissioned David Boag to create a pictorial record of the wildlife and habitats at the Group's European quarries. David visited all those operations, from the Western Isles of Scotland to the Channel Islands, and took some remarkable photographs. They were published as *Natural Quarry* and showed how both active and disused quarries can provide a vibrant environment for many species of wildlife as well as all manner of flora and fauna.

So well received was *Natural Quarry* that we commissioned David to undertake a similar project across our US operations. The much larger geographic spread - from Boston in the Northeast to Las Vegas in the Southwest - gave David a more diverse environmental canvas with which to work, but the results show the fascinating interaction between man and nature. Once again, he has produced some quite outstanding photographs.

Aggregate Industries commitment to environmental management is clear and unambiguous. We are fully certified to the international standard ISO 14001 in the UK and we will be certified in the US by April 2006. Our people are enthusiastic about the role they can play in not only minimising the environmental impact of our operations but, in many cases as this book shows, improving it.

Our thanks go to David for his hard work. I hope that you enjoy the results of his labour as much as I have.

Peter Tom
Group Chief Executive
Aggregate Industries plc

Mid Atlantic Region

The Aggregate Industries Mid Atlantic Region encompasses the Metropolitan Washington DC area, including parts of Maryland, Northern Virginia and West Virginia. The land that is managed by the company is wonderfully diverse, including open valleys, dense woodland and wide rivers. Both hard rock quarries and sand and gravel pits are in the region but most are difficult to observe as they tend be in remote locations or hidden from casual view by surrounding trees or woodland. Each quarry has a distinctive character of its own and provides a wealth of different habitats and accompanying wildlife.

The sand and gravel operation at La Plata, Maryland offers wide open views where the sky seems huge; like a canopy of blue that contrasts with the warm color of the sand.

When entering or leaving King George site in Virginia, truck drivers are treated to the sight of bright **trumpet creeper** flowers. The plants have become naturally established on the berms that border the entrance road and grow in profusion.

A mixture of wild flower seeds were scattered in an area of unused ground at an intersection of roads. The resulting flowers provide a colorful welcome to the quarry.

The dry soil in some parts of the site provides ideal growing conditions for the **wood lily**. Because it grows in a tall upright fashion the beautiful flowers are easy to spot.

Not every acre of land owned by Aggregate Industries is quarried. In many situations large areas of woodland are kept as a screen from roads or local houses. They are managed as havens for wildlife and become wonderful unspoiled places where the delightful tangle of vegetation encourages birds and insects, and provides shelter for mammals.

The sound of a **pileated woodpecker** striking a rotten tree stump, draws attention to the largest American woodpecker.

An old tree situated on the woodland edge provides a perfect nest location for a **Northern flicker**. Before the birds leave the nest they survey the area for danger. From their high vantage point they have an excellent view of the quarry activities.

The tangle
of lush
vegetation,
twisted
stems and
trailing
creepers,
creates a
jungle-like
habitat.

One major feature of quarrying is that the process does not use any chemicals that damage the environment. Unlike surrounding agricultural land, no herbicides or pesticides are used. As a result indigenous species of plants are able to flourish and become a food source for a wealth of different butterflies.

Eastern tiger swallowtail butterfly**.**

Pearl crescent butterfly.

Many species of butterflies make use of the damp quarry sand as a source of moisture. Here, a **spicebush swallowtail** extends its proboscis to take a drink.

Great spangled fritillary butterfly.

Common buckeye butterfly.

Having recently hatched from a chrysalis a **zebra swallowtail** butterfly rest in the heat of the sun.

Nature is quick to take advantage of any new situations. Although these slopes and benches have not yet been restored, trees and shrubs have already become established in the freshly revealed ground. Windblown seeds of **birch** and **cottonwood** trees rapidly take root and the vibrant fall colors contrast wonderfully against the gray rock face.

Some magnificent cliff faces have been created as a result of the quarry activity at Millville, West Virginia. Already plants have encroached into the nooks and crannies from the surrounding woods.

An exciting by-product of sand and gravel extraction is the areas of water that are created. Of course in some situations the land can be restored to agricultural use, but where it has been decided to leave it as a lake, it rapidly becomes a wonderful haven for wildlife. The most obvious creatures are the wealth of birds that are attracted into the area and as a huge flock of gulls arrive to bathe, drink and roost it is a breathtaking spectacle. However the lake is also a home for many less conspicuous animals.

A swirling mass of tiny **water beetles** creates an abstract pattern on the surface.

Empty shells are evidence of the large number of **molluscs** that thrive in the water.

Mid Atlantic Region

One feature of sand and gravel extraction is the need for settlement ponds or lakes. Water is used to clean the product and is then pumped into the lakes. The still water allows the sediment to settle to the bottom and clean water seeps out into the next pond down the line before it is recycled. The sediment is rich in nutrients and as a result plants rapidly become established and because no chemical additives are used in the process, the plants thrive. Of course the lakes quickly become choked with vegetation and the ponds need to be emptied regularly.

Natural patterns ripple across the sediment of a settlement pond.

Bright, fresh yellow **tickseed sunflowers** set a wonderful foreground for the still water of a settlement pond. They are typical of the many species of plants that use this habitat to flourish. The damp soil provides moisture for the plants all year round, even in the driest season.

At some stage a **rose** must have become established on the path that borders a settlement pond. It grew so prolifically that it now covers the whole of the bank, making the little track almost impassable.

Mid Atlantic Region

Floating leaves of aquatic plants cover large areas of a lake and a **spangled skimmer dragonfly** finds a place to rest.

Areas of land that were once quarried very quickly revert back to nature, either encouraged by quarry management, or naturally. They rapidly become little secret places for wildlife that are often secluded and private.

Many dramatic dragonflies are attracted to the still water. Once the underwater larval stage is complete the adults emerge from the water to hunt the area for other flying insects. A **calico pennant dragonfly** rest on a favourite perch.

The snare of a spider is set amongst the long grasses and the creature simply waits for a careless victim to stray into its trap. Despite its appearance this large and dramatic spider is harmless to humans and is commonly referred to as the **garden spider.**

Life in the wild and undisturbed corners of the quarry is like a miniature jungle. Where teeming invertebrates feed upon the plants and voracious predators use every method to catch and devour them.

Caterpillars come in all shapes and sizes; some are brightly colored indicating they are distasteful in an attempt to deter birds from eating them. Others are camouflaged in greens and browns, or are very hairy, once again to deter predators. The wealth of indigenous wild plants that surround the quarry provides an ample supply of food for these caterpillars, which in time will pupate and emerge as butterflies or moths.

Hundreds of different species of insects swarm in the dense vegetation. Many go unseen because they are small and insignificant. Grasshoppers and crickets are probably the most obvious of this teeming horde as they leap in all directions at the least disturbance.

Mid Atlantic Region

The variety of different habitats created by quarrying activities is astonishing. Even the lakes, which at first glance may look similar, vary in ways which suit different forms of plant and animal life. Some are very deep and therefore remain cold throughout the year, others are very shallow and warm and evaporate rapidly. One of the many considerations during restoration work, is how best to create and retain the variety, providing places that are not only pleasing to the eye, but also of value to wildlife.

A quiet and secret area
of marsh-land and water
that has long been
restored to nature.

Fish such as **carp** have managed to inhabit some of the quarry lakes. Presumably eggs were accidentally imported by birds.

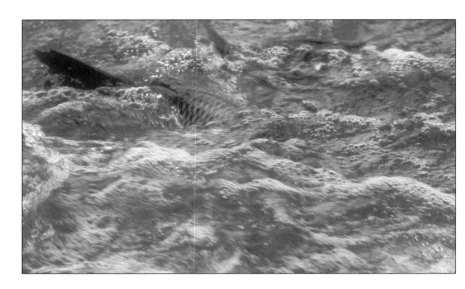

The Rappahannock River borders the King George sand and gravel site in Virginia and brings with it an added dimension. Tugboats regularly push barges along the river to transport products from the site. However, the river also brings wildlife right to the boundary. Birds in particular use the river as a highway and from their high elevation they quickly spot the quarry lakes only a few yards away.

The fish eating **osprey** has made use of a dolphin that the barges tie up to, as a location to nest. A pair has nested there for many years, successfully raising a brood of youngsters that try out their fishing abilities in the nearby quarry lakes.

Central Region

Aggregate Industries Central Region runs in a line across the southern half of Michigan down to Northern Indiana. It is a region of extremes, with bitter cold and biting winds in the winter, and dry scorching heat in the summer. For several months of the year the ground is locked with hard frost and lakes are sealed beneath inches of ice. But as life stirs in the spring the locations abound with the beauty of nature; from brightly coloured flowers to the songs of many birds.

Stockpiles of aggregate at the Chelsea site are covered with windswept snow creating a moonscape feeling of desolation. But it has a beauty of contrast; soft white snow and hard grey rock with sweeping hills and patterns of drifted snow.

Central Region

With its rusty-orange belly the **Eastern fox squirrel** is quite distinctive. It is a large tree squirrel that regularly can be seen crossing the tracks as it moves from one group of trees to another. It buries nuts in the ground to store and hide them for winter use. Of course it does not find them all again and that is the way many trees are introduced to the location.

Eastern chipmunks are common around the quarry perimeters. They are most easily seen in the autumn where their obsessive behaviour of collecting nuts makes them fearless of human activity. They use the store of food to survive the winter; waking from hibernation about every two weeks to feed from the larder.

Having taken a good meal from a rotting carcass, a pair of **turkey vultures** rest in the warmth of the sun to digest their meal. They arrive from the warmer climate in the south to breed in the region and mainly feed on road casualties.

NATURAL QUARRY

The shallow margins of lakes and settlement ponds are ideal habitats for several species of wading birds. The most common species to be found in the majority of quarries is the **killdeer**. They scamper around the quarry on their clockwork-like legs, oblivious of the huge vehicles. They use the berms as lookout perches from which they survey their domain. Most quarries echo to the calls of killdeer in the breeding season.

Overnight the appearance of the Wayland site is transformed by a fall of snow. The delicate flakes decorate every area, from the machinery and bare ground to the surrounding trees. At first glance it seems as if nature has come to a standstill, even a muffled silence pervades the area. However, a little investigation reveals footprints of cottontails, foxes and plenty of birds. Although the snow makes working conditions difficult for both humans and animal life alike, it is a beautiful sight to behold as the crystals of ice transform the mundane into the extraordinary.

During late summer, the Pullman site looks dry and parched in the heat of the midday sun. The air is still and the soil hard and cracked. This suits **tumbleweed** which is a plant of the open prairie. It gets its name from the fact that when mature it breaks at the roots, leaving the ball-shaped tangle of stems free. Driven by the wind it tumbles along, scattering thousands of seeds onto other areas of the site. It is particularly suited to disturbed, sandy soil but contrary to popular belief it is not actually an indigenous species, but a Russian invader.

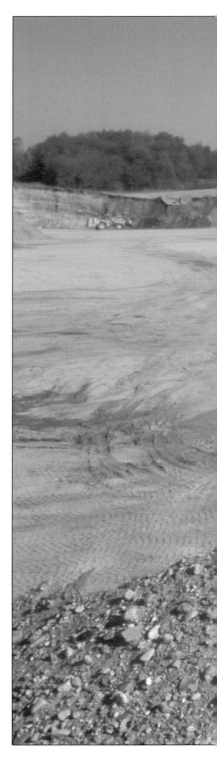

A **Blanding's turtle** finds itself in a rather strange environment. It rarely wanders far from marshes, bogs or lakes but possibly its damp habitat had dried up so it was forced to explore the area for a new home. Fortunately our operations create many such places and the turtle would not have far to roam at the Weyland site.

The **Blanding's turtle** is the only species with a bright yellow throat.

It is a common misconception that frogs live in ponds or lakes. In fact they only start their lives in water as a tadpole. Thereafter they roam freely, only returning to a pond to mate and spawn. **Leopard frogs** can be found a long distance from water but they are difficult to find because of their cryptic colors.

Hairy vetch is a plant that quickly colonises the bare soil. In some areas the beautiful blooms decorate the berms for a hundred yards or more.

Late summer brings a flush of bright yellow into the quarry as **sweet goldenrod** comes into flower. The distinctive smell of this plant makes it an easy species to identify and a crushed leaf produces a scent of liquorice.

Flowers of **spotted knapweed** can be found in almost all quarrying opperations. It is regarded as an agricultural weed but in a quarrying area it does no damage.

Chicory is an attractive flowering herb that is given credit for several medicinal properties. Although it is a wild plant it is often cultivated in gardens.

Growing up to three feet tall **bushy asters** brighten many quarry areas with their cheerful flowers. They produce flowers in a variety of colors from lavender through to white. It is a perennial species that flowers late in the year and as a result is often popular with butterflies that have few other flowers from which to feed at that time of year.

West Central Region

The obvious feature that dominates the West Central Region of Aggregate Industries is the Rocky Mountains, because the region is based around Denver, Colorado. The main hard rock quarries are actually tucked away in the foothills of the great mountain range. The sand and gravel workings are on the flat area of the plains, but even they are set within a backdrop of the magnificent mountains. The close proximity of the Rockies has a profound effect upon the wildlife and many species of both animal and plant life are discovered in the West Central Region that are not found in the other regions.

Because it is located in the foothills of the Rocky Mountains it is possible to get a high elevation view of Morrison Quarry. The high benches, steep slopes and dramatic scenery make it one of the most spectacular hard rock quarries.

NATURAL QUARRY   67

Although not brightly colored the **gray jay** is a very attractive bird; its pale, soft gray, fluffy plumage makes it very appealing. Like other jays, it is an inquisitive and bold bird that quickly learns to make use of new habitats and opportunities.

In this region the **Steller's jay** replaces the more well know blue jay. The vibrant blue belly, wings and tail make it easily identifiable. It is at home in the surrounding conifer trees but will often enter the heart of the quarry as it scavenges for food.

Clearly wildlife does not view things in the way humans do. At the Distel Site there is a large area where the **black-tailed prairie dogs** can expand and populate without any disturbance, but each year they burrow closer. This family are being raised in a burrow which the adults had dug only three feet from the main road into the site. This is one of the busiest areas, where trucks often line up for the scale house.

The distant Rocky Mountain peaks of Meeker and Longs Peak are almost duplicated by the mountains of aggregate in the quarry stockpile.

Snow covered peaks form a backdrop to the activity at the Distel location. The site itself is situated in a flat area of sand and gravel. Here the weather is hot, fresh leaves on the trees display that spring has arrived. Dandelions have not only flowered but have even produced their feathery seeds. Only 30 miles west, winter clings to the high mountain rocks and little vegetation grows.

Like the antlers of a buck fall to the ground each year, this old dead tree will soon topple and fall.

Elk roam freely through some of the quarry land, entering and leaving as the fancy takes them. During the fall the 'bugle' calls of the bulls, as they threaten rivals, echo around the site. In this way the bulls attempt to maintain their harem of cows

A splendid bull **elk** supports a fine head of antlers.

The Distel location has become a regular roost for a magnificent bird, the **American pelican.** Although birds are present throughout the day, numbers increase during the late afternoon. Drifting out of the blue sky they settle on the lake. At first they sail on the water, preening, but it is not long before they begin to gather on a little island where they settle to roost for the night.

Where sand and gravel has been removed from the land, the depression in the ground rapidly fills with water. Scanning across this area it is easy to envisage its potential as a beautiful wildlife habitat. In some respects it is like gardening on a massive, long-term scale. However, nature will not wait and even before the machines have moved out, plants and animal life begin to encroach.

The Rocky Mountains form a backdrop to all of the quarries in the region. They are the horizon for many beautiful landscapes in the area.

Although not brightly colored the **American avocet** is a most attractive bird. The subtle rust color of its head and neck blend into pristine black-and-white plumage. Slender, and elegant in its movements, it sweeps the water with its long up-curved bill.

The **greater yellowlegs** is a visitor on its migration route from its northern breeding range to its wintering area in the warmer south.

This **evening primrose**, with its very large white flowers, spreads by underground roots and is often abundant on steep dry slopes with light soil. The flower is very large for the size of the rest of the plant.

Plants of semi-desert, **prickly pears** are common in the higher parts of the hardrock quarries.

Barrel cacti are especially suited to rocky slopes, which explains its prevalence in Lyons Quarry.

Warm rocks, dry ground and plenty of cracks and crevices create the perfect habitat for **prairie rattlesnakes**. Although it is not a regular occurrence, many of our workers have a story to tell about their confrontation with a 'rattler'. Probably some of the tales are a little exaggerated, because rattle snakes are quite secretive and not looking for trouble. Nevertheless good numbers are active in the quarries in the foothills of the Rocky Mountains.

A **violet-green swallow** settles between the barbs of a wire fence.

It is a common misconception that birds prefer areas of green; natural and wild places. In fact their requirements are very simple; a good supply of food and water, and a secure place to nest and roost. A suitable hunting or song perch need not be a green branch of a tree; wire fences and posts provide an equally good vantage point. As a result quarries provide everything many birds require.

A **lark sparrow** is framed in a wire mesh fence.

A **great crested flycatcher** on a barbed wire fence at the new Thornton location.

A **Western meadowlark** uses a concrete post as a song perch.

Mountain bluebirds have favorite bushes on which they perch as they survey the ground below for food. They look stunning as the sun catches their plumage.

One cannot help finding **ruby-throated hummingbirds** tiny stature and iridescent color most appealing. But it is its amazing manoeuvrability and speed that leaves one feeling breathless.

As its name implies, the **house finch** is a bird that is often associated with human habitation. The males flush of bright red on its head and chest makes it a distinctive species as it forages for a variety of seeds.

NATURAL QUARRY

The foothills of the Rocky Mountains is the favored habitat of **mule deer**. Therefore it is hardly surprising that they are regularly found wandering along the quarry tracks. Mule deer are especially prolific in the various quarries of the region during the winter. They are driven down from the colder slopes of the Rocky Mountains by the snow and freezing conditions, to find shelter and food in the more mild conditions of the foothills. The deer that reside in the quarry have become very used to the activity of people and machines. They take little notice of passing trucks barely lifting their heads to watch them.

Prior to sand and gravel extraction, a survey was carried out and a total of 70 species of mammals, birds, reptiles and amphibians were found. After the work was completed the land was restored and there were in excess of 210 species present - 3 times as many! It is now a beautiful nature reserve known as South Platte Park, with a large lake, a cycle path and footpath. The dramatic increase in the wildlife population was brought about by the formation of the large lake, but equally valuable was the creation of a wetland habitat.

Cattail flourishes around the margin of the lake. Their distinctive seed-head looks solid and hard but it is made up of thousands of tiny seeds that will eventually drift away on the breeze.

Huge pods burst open on the **milkweed plant** to reveal a mass of seed. Attached to each seed is a fluffy, white awn that catches the wind and carries the seed to a new area.

Creating an area of wetland was felt to be of uppermost importance when restoring this part of South Platte Park. The result was not only pleasing to the eye but it also increased the population of animal and plant species dramatically.

Large numbers of **crayfish** can be found in some of the lakes. It is difficult to imagine how they manage to populate some locations because they are completely separated from established, natural waterways.

High above Morrison Quarry the atmosphere is constantly changing. The same landscape provides a fascinating variety of images depending on the sun, the cloud and the rain. Only the sound of a breeze cutting through course vegetation and the song of birds can be heard in this remote and wild corner of the quarry.

White swirls of cloud sweep in from the mountains and engulf the quarry, leaving every twig, stem and flower decorated with drops of rain. The cloud obliterates distant views, and trees become eerie silhouettes. Total silence pervades and the air is filled with the delightful smells of surrounding herbs.

This **racoon** had a very disturbed sleep during the day because it chose to rest under the eaves at South Platte Park.

Many **Eastern cottontails** are resident in the quarries. They seem perfectly content in areas where the vegetation seems sparse to human eyes.

A **rock squirrel** pops its head over a berm to observe a passing quarry vehicle.

The **red fox** is to be found in almost every quarry but it is shy, and therefore is not often seen. However, as with many young mammals, the cubs are often inquisitive and have not learned to fear humans especially in areas where they have become used to the quarry activity.

A **golden-mantled ground squirrel** found in a quiet part of Deer Creek Quarry.

The fall colors reflect in the tumbling river that runs along the boundary of the Lyons Quarry. The little river flows only a few paces from the busy workshops and scale house with its constant stream of trucks. But to glance over the bank towards the river, magically takes you into a different world.

The **American Dipper** is a bird that specializes in fast flowing water. They go underwater to find hidden insect larvae, therefore they nest close to their source of food; in a crevice that overlooks the water.

The river is bordered by the quarry on one side and high cliffs on the other. The noise of tumbling and rushing water, as it crashes over boulders, constantly accompanies the activity in the quarry.

Snow exaggerates the high rock faces and
well worn tracks of Morrison Quarry.

The Northeast Region extends across Massachusetts and New Hampshire. The contrast between the busy activity of the quarries close to Boston and the peaceful solitude of the more remote locations is reflected in the wildlife. Therefore each quarry has a distinct character of its own. The location also ensures that there are contrasting seasonal differences, with cold winters, balmy summer months and of course the wonderful colors of fall.

Right in the deepest part of Swampscott Quarry is a miniature nature reserve. At first it seems a most unlikely place to find such a wealth of wild plants because it is totally surrounded by quarry workings. The dramatic backdrops of towering cliffs seem to exaggerate this remarkable little wild haven.

Surely the **Northern cardinal** is one of the most bright and most easily recognized birds. It is only the males that have such a vibrant plumage although the females still show a tinge of red in their olive feathers.

American robins are residents in the region and are commonly found investigating any short cropped grassland and damp areas. They are mainly searching for worms and other invertebrates that inhabit the quarry.

While some birds in the quarry are bright and colorful, others are more dramatic. The huge wingspan and gliding flight of **turkey vultures** can be seen over most quarries of the region in the summer.

Wherever trees are abundant it is certain that **Eastern gray squirrels** will be resident and quarries are no exception.

Apparently **domesticated goats** were released from a nearby military base several years ago. They were allowed to roam freely and one has taken up residence in Littleton Quarry.

Making use of its camouflaged colours an **Eastern cottontail** hides in the long vegetation beside a quarry road.

The **Eastern chipmunk** is a cheeky little character that can appear in almost any quarry. Its underground burrow usually opens out on a slope or bank therefore it often uses established berms.

It is probably Taunton Quarry that creates and preserves some of the most valuable habitat in the region. At one time large areas of the region would have been swamp and bogs, however, much of this has been drained for agricultural use. The remaining pockets of swampland have become havens for the wildlife that had free roam of the area; in particular amphibians, turtles, dragonflies and other insects.

But the atmosphere of the marshy habitat is also unique, with a wonderful mixture of shrubs, bushes and trees. Shallow pools of still water give off the scent of rotting leaves and every pond reflects the overhanging canopy of twigs.

NATURAL QUARRY   111

NATURAL QUARRY   115

Northeast Region

The Ashland Quarry is covered in snow and even the roads and tracks have disappeared beneath the deep covering. However, the **white-tailed deer** still knows exactly where its trails are hidden and it follows its regular route to its favorite feeding area. The quarry is surrounded by forest that provides plenty of cover for the deer and the rough areas of ground provide ample food.

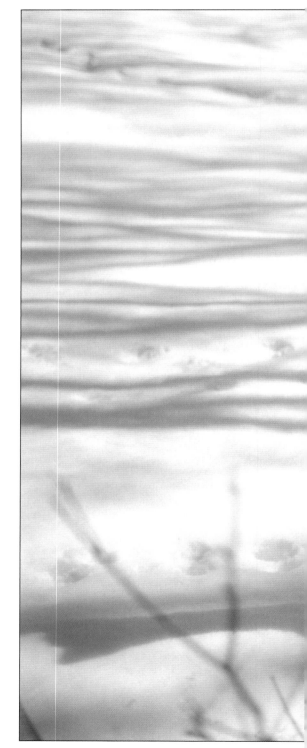

Every twig, stem and branch is decorated by the heavy fall of snow. Although it can be an inconvenience and a familiar occurrence, it is nevertheless an amazing transformation of the landscape that only nature could produce on such a grand scale.

Not only does the fall produce vibrant colors in the changing leaves, it also is the season of colorful berries and fruits. For many of us the arrival of fall means the end of the year; the time when plants die. But in fact it is the beginning, as the new generation of seeds, nuts, fruits, hips, acorns and berries are produced by plants. This is a natural harvest for the many creatures that feed on them.

Birds and mammals consider it to be a bonanza of food that enables them to put on body weight in preparation for the difficult months of winter that lie ahead. The trees and shrubs rely upon the birds and mammals to do the work of dispersing the seed; and so it is an effective symbiotic relationship.

The colors of a **monarch butterfly** compare to the colors of the fall leaves. It is widespread throughout America and often feeds on the asters that can be found in the quarries in the fall.

Overlooking the quarry red **maple trees** change into seasonal colors. Seen individually the leaves may look tatty and worn but the overall effect can be breathtaking.

A single **staghorn sumac** has established itself in the bottom of Swampscott Quarry. Before the leaves fall they change to a delightful range of yellows and reds.

Virginia creeper trials across a wet rock. The contrast in texture and color gives an added interest to this common plant.

A **bronze frog** rests in a shallow part of a settlement pond.

Leopard frogs leave the water and explore the surrounding area in search of prey.

Spotted turtles are especially fond of the bogs and swamps that surround some of the more established lakes. They can sometimes be seen scurrying across the quarry roads as they move from one pond to the next.

Wetland habitats provided by quarries are valuable assets to the area. They double the number of species of both animal and plant life that are able to flourish.

The **Eastern ribbon snake** is very agile and fast. It is semi aquatic, feeding on small frogs, fish and salamanders. They are also found absorbing the warmth from the aggregate on the quarry tracks.

Downy woodpeckers are non-migratory birds and so need to be able to cope with the difficulties of winter. They feed upon insects throughout the year and the task of finding them after a fall of snow seems daunting. But they are well designed to chisel and chip away at the bark of trees where they find hibernating insects tucked away in the cracks and crevices. They have learned to exploit the generosity of people and regularly visit backyard feeders to take suet.

A landscape of white hides the stockpiles of aggregate and sand. It covers the frozen lakes and conceals the tracks and roads that thread through the quarry bottom. Sounds that usually echo around the rock faces become muffled by the soft snow and the quarry becomes strangely silent.

NATURAL QUARRY

North Central Region

Minnesota claims to be the state of 10,000 lakes and there can be little doubt that water plays an important role in the wildlife and natural beauty of the quarries of Aggregate Industries North Central Region. The region also extends beyond the bounds of Minnesota into the wide open prairie lands of North Dakota. Thus the habitats and interest in this area is extremely varied.

Barges loaded with sand wait for tug boats to guide them effortlessly down the River Mississippi. Both the Nelson site and Larson Quarry use the river as a highway to transport products. It is a very environmentally acceptable method of transport.

Standing motionless in its own reflection a **great blue heron** waits patiently for a meal. The quarry lakes have become stocked with fish and the heron is aware of the easy pickings.

Snowy white plumage and elegant movements typify the **great egret.** The long slender neck acts like a whiplash as the bird stabs and grabs at fish. One can't help wondering at its ability to allow for the angle of refraction on the water surface.

Standing tall on the edge of a lake a **milkweed** plant is the foreground for the activities at the Nelson site. This species is a source of food for the caterpillars of the monarch butterfly. Later in the year it will produce large pods that release thousands of feathery seeds.

Black-eyed Susan is a native plant of the prairies that seems to enjoy the dry sandy soil of the quarry roads and berms. It flowers throughout the summer, bringing splashes of color into many areas of the quarry.

A huge embankment at the St. Croix location was recently restored. During the summer an amazing variety of wild flowers appeared on the new ground. They including bright yellow **birdsfoot trefoil,** deep purple **musk thistles** and cheerful **oxeye daisies**. Of course as a result of so many wild plants the vegetation was alive with grasshoppers, crickets and other insects.

Dry grassy hillside is the preferred habitat of **purple prairie clover** and so the restored land suited this species to perfection.

A single **black-eyed Susan** provides a feed for a butterfly known as a **silvery checkerspot.**

Aptly named, **butterfly weed** lived up to its reputation and was covered with **gray copper butterflies**. It grew so close to the road that each time a vehicle went past the butterflies left in a cloud of wings, returning within a few moments.

At first glance it is difficult to imagine that this waterfall is not natural but flows from a large culvert that carries the water. It has all the qualities of a natural waterfall, with algae, lichens and plants that enjoy the constant water splash. The rushing, tumbling noise is also familiar as the water thunders onto the worn rocks at its base. Standing in the spray of the fall, it is difficult to imagine that one is actually in an active mining site.

A **beaver** tows a sprig of
willow back to the lodge.

Clambering onto the bank, a beaver feeds on the lush vegetation.

One can't help wondering if the beavers had bitten off more than they could chew!

Although the **American beaver** is mainly nocturnal they can often be observed at dawn and dusk. They do not like to be disturbed by humans and so quiet lakes in quarries provide perfect sanctuaries, such as one on the site known as Pit 21. Their ability to fell trees is well known and it is claimed that a 5 inch thick willow can be felled in only 3 minutes. The bark and leaves are eaten, but the branches are used to create their familiar dams and large lodges that can be seen on many similar lakes.

A small backwater of a beaver lake.

Evidence of beaver activity can be found in plenty of quarries throughout the regions.

NATURAL QUARRY

The road leading down to the workshops at the Redwing Quarry is decorated with wild flowers. The track is like an opening in the woodland, allowing light to penetrate for the smaller flowering plants. **Wild columbine** and **wild geranium** are amongst the many species that are quick to take advantage of the situation.

A close inspection reveals the intricate design of the **wild columbine** flower.

Surely the most awesome bird to be found in any quarry is the American national bird; the **bald eagle**. They can often be seen sitting on the numerous berms or pieces of machinery around the Nelson site but the most popular perch is a telegraph pole right in the entrance to Larson Quarry.

Quite often a first sign of this majestic bird is a great shadow that sweeps across the ground; glancing up, the 7 foot wingspan can hardly be missed. The young birds take 4 or 5 years to achieve the adult plumage and so many of the eagles in the quarries are still in juvenile plumage.

They feed mainly on fish which they catch either from the quarry lakes or the nearby River Mississippi. They will also feed on carrion, although one cant help wondering at the safety of the Canada geese goslings that are reared on the lakes.

The Nelson site is on Grey Cloud Island in the River Mississippi and looking across the water the wonderful rich colors of fall are breathtaking. A **great blue heron** stands in a mirror of the season, as the vibrant colours are reflected in the still water.

Even in the most apparently inhospitable areas plants manage to germinate and grow. Provided they are able to establish a root system quickly that reaches down to a supply of water they will rapidly become established. Even if they should die their effort is not wasted. The decomposing plant will add to the humus which will retain a little moisture, giving a better opportunity for another seed to develop the following season.

The rotting stump of a fallen tree is host to many types of fungi. The fungi help with the important process of decomposition. As the stump rots, it releases nutrients for the next generation of plants.

Several years ago at the Nelson property, a tall pole was erected with the cooperation of Aggregate Industries, and a secure platform was attached to the top. It was part of a reintroduction program for **ospreys**, because they had been lost from the area for many years. The intention was to create a suitable platform for ospreys to nest when they returned from their winter migration to South America. The experiment was clearly successful because very quickly the birds accepted the potential nest site, carrying in plenty of twigs and branches and laying a clutch of eggs.

It is an ideal nest site because the property is surrounded by water; in fact it is an island in the River Mississippi, known as Grey Cloud Island. The lakes on the site also contain fish that are the source of food for these dramatic birds.

Since 1999 the ospreys have returned to nest on the high platform where they have raised at least seven young over the past few years.

The high nest platform gives the ospreys an unhindered all-round view of the area. They can see across the River Mississippi, the site and the lakes.

The reintroduction of the osprey into the area has been very successful due to the cooperation of landowners and last season there were 35 active nests.

A backwater of the River Mississippi spills into the quarry land.
It has a secret and wild atmosphere where only turtles, dragonflies and other water loving creatures live.

The still water of quarry ponds and lakes provide perfect habitats for many species of dragonflies including a **twelve spotted skimmer.**

Painted turtles are extremely sensitive to movement and at the slightest sign of danger they slip into the water. As a result, although many quarry lakes have large numbers of turtles, they are difficult to observe.

Southwest Region

Aggregate Industries Southwest Region is typified by the searing heat and harsh environment of the Mojave desert of Nevada. The region revolves around the glamour and excitement of Las Vegas, but the raw beauty of the surrounding mountains and desert are never far away. The first impression of the quarries is that they are barren places, but even here a variety of life can be discovered.

Yucca plants provide a foreground to almost every view of the Sloan Mountain Quarry and Summerlin sand and gravel site. It is a plant that symbolizes the region and has adapted perfectly to the harsh desert environment.

Southwest Region

There is a wonderful variety of cacti surrounding the quarries of the region. A walk across the desert reveals cacti of many different intricate shapes and sizes. Of course the beauty of their shape and size can be outweighed by the wickedly sharp spines.

Pencil cholla release their spines at the slightest touch. This brought about a myth suggesting that it jumps if you step on its roots; embedding its spines into you!

The **beavertail cactus** only has short bristles and produces stunning, bright blooms in the spring.

Hedgehog cactus produce bright strawberry-red blooms, giving rise to its other name of **strawberry hedgehog**.

As **barrel cacti** grow they tend to lean towards the south so that they expose the minimum surface to the hot mid-day sun.

When the flowers of **silver cholla** first appear they are green, but as they mature they become yellow.

At ones approach **side-blotched lizards** scamper for cover beneath tufts of vegetation or into holes in the ground. They are extremly abundant in the quarry and are active for most of the year.

Although **desert tortoises** are the largest reptiles in the area, they are very difficult to find. It is an endangered species that has declined dramatically over the last decade and is therefore protected by law. Although they can live for up to 100 years feeding upon the sparse vegetation, they are slow to breed and most of the little hatchlings do not survive to maturity. It is the Nevada state reptile and much is being done to ensure it does not fade to extinction. They amble through the desert to the margins of the quarry.

The **Western whiptail lizard** is very long and slender with a distinctive pointed snout.

At first glance the desert seems colorless; a landscape of gray and dull brown. But one cannot view the desert from a distance; you have to be involved. During the spring, a hike through the scrub vegetation soon reveals a multitude of flowers.

One of the larger and more obvious flowers is **Indian or desert paintbrush**. It is a perennial plant that has a long flowering season.

Little bright red flowers along a tall slender stem indicates a **globe mallow** plant. Some small plants may produce a single stem while others form into little bushy clumps.

Mojave aster.

Yellow cups.

The setting sun highlights the bright **brittlebush** flowers scattered amongst the quarry boulders.

One of the most prolific shrubs in the quarry is the **creosote bush**. It typifies the desert, being able to withstand the hot and dry conditions. The bright yellow flowers may appear from March until June and brighten many corners of the quarry property. Given enough moisture they can grow quite tall but conditions here limit its growth to about four feet.

The quarries are situated in a treeless landscape where the **yucca** is the tallest plant. Although they can grow to a height of 16 feet, most plants are less than half that height within the quarry region. A wealth of bell-shaped flowers burst from the centre of the shrub in spring. The long spear-like leaves are very distinctive and it is the yucca that stands out most amongst the desert plants.

Wild burro were introduced into the area to be used as pack animals. They have an amazing ability to lose up to thirty percent of their weight due to water loss and then replenish it in only five minutes drinking. This meant that many burros outlived their owners who died in this hot and arid terrain. Thus, many years ago, the wild population developed which roam the desert today. They cover large distances as they wander in search of the sparse vegetation and occasionally come down from the surrounding hills into the quarry area. They have little fear of humans and seem unconcerned by the activity. The females usually have one colt a year and they may live to be 25.

Wandering across the quarry land it is quickly apparent that there are many holes burrowed into the ground. The owners of these holes tend to be rather secretive and quickly scamper underground at your approach. But a close view of a **white-tailed antelope squirrel** reveals a cheeky little character that is well designed for the habitat. It feeds on a variety of vegetation, including seeds from the yucca plants; it will also catch insects such as grasshoppers.

Looking from the Summerlin site towards the distant mountains, a small outcrop of red rock indicates its proximity to the Red Rock Canyon conservation area.

A rare downpour of rain carves a rivulet through the desert. However, the parched soil soon absorbs the welcome moisture and the scorching heat ensure it is only temporary.

A **painted lady butterfly** rests on the ground absorbing the warmth of the late evening sun.

A dry river bed borders an entrance to the site. It has been without water for so long that scrubby plants have taken root in the gravel soil.

NATURAL QUARRY

Looking in one direction from Sloan Mountain the natural light begins to fade as the sun sets in the sky. While in the other direction the artificial lights of Las Vegas now illuminate the night.

The bright lights of the Las Vegas 'Strip' far below the quarry, symbolize the wealth of the city and the purpose of a quarry in the middle of a desert. The whole city seems to revolve around this one street where money lost on green baize gambling tables or dropped into 'slots' funds a whole community.

Index